PRAISE FOR *HE SAID, SHE SAID: BRANDING*

The intriguing "he said, she said" tango between Michael and Jaci give their audience an inside look into over twenty years of creativity and strategy. They make the critical connection that a brand is about connection. By sharing their story, Michael and Jaci exemplify the importance of being relatable, which makes *He Said, She Said: Branding* a shining example of how to capture your target audience.

Often misled by branding myths, entrepreneurs typically ask the wrong questions in their customer discovery process. *He Said, She Said: Branding* debunks these myths and provides the right questions to validate customer perception. Additionally, Michael and Jaci define not only what a brand is—but most importantly, what it is not. Spoiler alert: it is not a logo.

– Destin Ortego
Executive director of Opportunity Machine

T0124501

Ying and Yang is a concept of dualism. The proven idea that two opposite things can complement each other. Nothing better describes the relationship of Michael & Jaci. They give rise to each other professionally by connecting yet being interdependent. What a great read on making a marriage work, at work.

– *Michele & Sean Ezell*
Founders and *owners of Tsunami Restaurants (Lafayette, New Orleans, Baton Rouge)*

It doesn't matter who said it, you have to dive into this book for a fun and informative exploration of personal and professional brand building filled with actionable anecdotes. Love the Russo Five Rs technique! And that's what I say.

– *Park Howell*
The world's most industrious storyteller
Founder, The Business of Story

Jaci and Michael Russo's book, **He Said, She Said: Branding,** *explains better than anyone else how to take the equal parts of creative design and marketing strategy to create an appealing brand.* The book not only communicates the importance of branding, but also how to apply these branding principles into traditional and more accepted methods of advertising. It articulates a unique process, a five-phase methodology that provides marketing practitioners a clear-cut branding road map.

This book is an easy read and is filled with practical advice and personal examples of their dynamic process for branding. As a business development consultant to over 450 advertising agencies across the US, Canada, and Europe, Jaci and Michael are two of the best branding experts that I've ever worked with. I highly recommend their book."

– Michael Gass
Founder and owner, Fuel Lines Business Development

HE SAID SHE SAID

BRANDING

MICHAEL RUSSO & JACI RUSSO

HE SAID, SHE SAID:
BRANDING

MICHAEL RUSSO & JACI RUSSO

Advantage®

Published by Advantage, Charleston, South Carolina.
Member of Advantage Media Group.

ADVANTAGE is a registered trademark, and the Advantage colophon is a trademark of Advantage Media Group, Inc.

Printed in the United States of America.

10 9 8 7 6 5 4 3 2 1

ISBN: 978-1-64225-193-7
LCCN: 2021901632

Book design by Michael Russo

This publication is designed to provide accurate and authoritative information in regard to the subject matter covered. It is sold with the understanding that the publisher is not engaged in rendering legal, accounting, or other professional services. If legal advice or other expert assistance is required, the services of a competent professional person should be sought.

Advantage Media Group is proud to be a part of the Tree Neutral® program. Tree Neutral offsets the number of trees consumed in the production and printing of this book by taking proactive steps such as planting trees in direct proportion to the number of trees used to print books. To learn more about Tree Neutral, please visit **www.treeneutral. com**.

Advantage Media Group is a publisher of business, self-improvement, and professional development books and online learning. We help entrepreneurs, business leaders, and professionals share their Stories, Passion, and Knowledge to help others Learn & Grow. Do you have a manuscript or book idea that you would like us to consider for publishing? Please visit **advantagefamily.com** or call **1.866.775.1696**.

To all the business owners, entrepreneurs, and true believers who entrusted us with their brands:

Thank you.

FOREWORD

For those working in marketing and advertising, this should be the best of all possible times. Thanks to advances in digital technology, you know how much of your money to spend on marketing, exactly where to put it, and what your ROI will be. Not only that, you can tell which messaging is working. In real time. And if something isn't working, you can just change it on the fly.

I'll pause here to allow you to stop laughing or, perhaps, to recover from your fit of rage.

Yes, digital technology has brought a lot of good to marketing. Things can be done faster. Collaboration is easier. And targeting is much more precise. You can hit people with an ad while they're searching for the products or services you sell. You can hit people with an ad on websites relevant to your brand. You can even more precisely target TV spots these days.

These are good things. I came up in print journalism so it pains me to say this, but it's a lot better to reach a consumer with a fairly cheap digital ad while they read a website than it is to spend hundreds of thousands on a print campaign that may be seen only by the bird in the cage it lines.

Yet, marketers and agencies still struggle. Why? Because all the technology in the world will only get you so far if you don't have the fundamentals down. And the most fundamental thing for a brand is, well, the branding. It's almost depressing how many marketing professionals forget that part. And I'm continually amazed at people who think an ad campaign can patch over the gaps in a poorly built-out brand.

The book you hold in your hands—or the book that's on the e-reader you're holding in your hands— is one about fundamentals. It reconnects you to the bedrock of branding, reminding you of some old lessons while teaching you a lot of new ones. And it does so in a rather clever manner. By starting off with their own story, Jaci and Michael show you how brandRUSSO was built before telling you about the fundamentals necessary for building your own.

This is a book about identifying your personality and shaping it. It's about balancing creativity and strategy and forging emotional connections. It's about laying down a foundation before you rush out and start spending on media, whether it be traditional or digital. It's a process that should work for your company, regardless of size, industry, or location.

You'll find strategy here. You'll find tactics. And you'll see how the fundamentals have changed in the wake of new media technology and customer behaviors. You may have heard that the consumer is in control. But have you internalized it? Jaci and Michael have made it the first of their 5 Rs: Realize the consumer owns your brand.

You'll have to read the book to see what the other 5 Rs are. I'm not here to do your homework. But rest assured there are plenty of concrete examples and, just as important, the questions you need to ask yourself to apply the lessons to your own business.

They manage to relay all this in plain English, rather than the overly jargonized nonsense that too many ad people speak these days. And get this. They don't always agree on everything. (If you're smarter than me, you might have figured this out by the title of the book.) It's a rare thing to see coauthors voicing their differences over the nuances of their own marketing philosophy. It's refreshing and honest and shines a light on how marketing actually works.

As a bonus, Jaci and Michael are funny as hell. I don't read a lot of industry books, and that's in large part because when it comes time to put pen to paper, too many people forget they're working in one of the most fun and creative industries around. That exec you can spend three hours laughing with over beers is suddenly doing a bad impersonation of your least favorite professor.

This is not that.

So enjoy the book. Laugh, learn, and—who knows—make a killing.

—*Ken Wheaton*
former Editor of Advertising Age*, content strategist, author of* "Duck Duck Gator" *and other novels.*

INTRODUCTION

What do coins, marriage, and branding have in common? It might sound like a trick question or even a senseless riddle, but there's an answer (and a point to be made): they all have duality. Two sides to a coin, two people in a marriage, and two parts of branding.

One can't live without the other. But what does duality in branding actually mean?

That's just one of the many topics we're going to discuss in this book, because duality is absolutely critical to a brand's success.

So are the basic principles of branding.

So is understanding the thought process behind creating a successful brand.

And so is understanding what branding is, what

it is not, and what it could do for your company and its bottom line.

We're Michael and Jaci Russo—cofounders of brandRUSSO, a strategic branding agency. In this book, we'll share our thoughts on branding, our process, and the story of how it all came to be.

But for now, we just want to say how glad we are that this book made its way into your hands—because whether you're looking to brand your company, learn about branding in the twenty-first century, or figure out what branding even means, you've come to the right place.

Often, the branding process goes something like this: a company hires a traditional agency (or Billy, the nephew of its CEO's sister's brother) who lures them in with a lot of fancy industry talk and shelves full of shiny awards. Said agency (or Billy) convinces the client that they have the magic answer to all the company's problems.

After all is said and done, the company is left wondering if they gained anything apart from a hefty bill.

That's usually when our phone rings.

"What do we do?" clients ask. "We don't have much of a budget left. We spent it. Now what?"

 Jaci: When I travel the country for speaking engagements and to teach workshops, the conversation is disturbingly similar: "I know I'm wasting fifty percent of my advertising budget, but I don't know which half." Our answer: probably both halves. Simply having a pretty picture or a beautiful brochure isn't enough. You have to dig deeper and work harder to connect with your audience.

At the same time, you don't have to hire huge multimillion-dollar companies to get the results you want and deserve. There are branding agencies out there that do exceptional work and can get you a much better return on your investment at a fraction of the cost.

But how do you tell the fakes from the for-reals?

Welcome to our book and the brandRUSSO story. The first piece of advice we'll give you along those lines is this: before branding can save you, you have to know what it actually is and means. Truth is, knowledge is your greatest superpower in the branding world. And having that knowledge can help save you time and money on ineffective efforts.

This book is our avenue to demonstrating what's worked well for us over the course of our twenty years in the industry while empowering you with the information you need to make informed decisions. By the time you finish this book, our hope is that you'll be able to identify what a strong branding process looks like, how to make confident choices for your brand, and where you may have missed the mark in previous branding endeavors.

On this branding journey, we'll stick by your side, showing you the ins and outs of branding from a his-and-her viewpoint (duality at its best!).

The journey will be fun, fast, and full of insights. So strap on your seatbelts and get ready for the ride.

In good cheer,

Michael & Jaci Russo

CHAPTER 1: IT STARTED AT TGI FRIDAY'S

We're married … and we work together. I know. That's a mic-drop sentence right there. The one that draws surprised looks, blank expressions, and curious stares that scream, "You do what?"

Those six words spark a myriad of questions for most people.

Seriously? A husband and wife working *together*?

How do you do it?

How do you see each other at work and home and then raise a family together without constantly being at each other's throats?

How are you both still *alive*?

When COVID-19 hit and the entire nation was forced to shelter in place, working remotely alongside spouses, everyone got a small taste of our daily lives.

Thing is, we've been doing it for twenty years, and while it's not a cakewalk, we've found ways to make it work. Sure, there are times our marriage edges its way into an occasional business meeting, and that's often when things get interesting.

Like the time Michael threw a water bottle at me during a production meeting. He swears he "lightly tossed" it in my direction in response to the look I threw him for squeezing it repeatedly (one of the most annoying things imaginable, might I add).

Michael: I didn't throw it at her, I tossed it. And for the record, the bottle was empty.

Jaci: I politely asked him to put the bottle down, and he threw it at me. Overhand. That's not a toss, it's a throw.

For better or for worse, that's kind of how we operate, with two very different recollections of any incident—including how we first met and created one of our proudest accomplishments (outside of our four kids), our agency: brandRUSSO.

She Said: From LA to LA and Back Again

Growing up in Lafayette, Louisiana, I spent a lot of time with my grandmother Bernardine. She was by far one of the classiest, smartest, and (dare I say) coolest people I've ever known. She was my role model and my mentor, and when I went to her seeking advice on whether I should leave college and move to Los Angeles to chase my dreams, she didn't hesitate. "I'll miss you, but go," she said. So, three years into school, I quit my bartending job, packed up my Alfa Romeo convertible with everything I owned, and drove across the country to the city of palm trees, beaches, and Hollywood.

My time in LA was challenging, exciting, and formative—giving me the opportunity to meet and work with many amazing and influential people. It started with a stint at CAA (Creative Artist Agency), where I worked with A-list actors and actresses. After that, I went out on my own to help form a multi-media company, L2 Communications. One of our first projects was the Denzel Washington and Russell Crow film *Virtuosity*. It was after that, when I took on a challenging role as the executive assistant to media mogul Barry Diller, that I began understanding the significant role branding played across all mediums.

But as life often does, it threw me a curveball: my grandmother became sick. And just as quickly as I'd decided to move to LA, I was packed and headed back home to Louisiana. It was hard to not only leave LA but to also leave a thriving career that I had invested so much time in. But the move ended up being one of the best decisions I ever made. Looking back, I'm so grateful I made that choice, because Bernardine passed away a year later, and I got to spend the last days of her life by her side.

And I'm also grateful for another reason. Now, for a natural-born storyteller, Michael doesn't like long-winded details when it comes to anything, not even the story of how we first met. But details are what I'm all about (plus, pissing him off is fun).

It started at a Louisiana ad agency's Christmas party, where I noticed a familiar face in the crowd. I didn't have anything to lose except my curiosity, but he was the one who ended up approaching me at the end of the night just as he was leaving. (He remembers this differently than me, to say the least, but we'll talk about that later.)

"Hey," I said. "Are you by chance Melissa's friend?"

And that's how I "officially" met Michael Russo. Turned out my best friend from college, Melissa, who was also a sorority sister of mine, was one of his close friends as well. Michael and Melissa performed together in college, and while I'd seen him onstage a few times, we'd never actually met. Anyway, I shared our meeting with Melissa, who was living in Seattle at the time, and after confiding in her that I needed a date for an upcoming Mardi Gras ball, she replied, "Why don't you ask Michael? He owns a tux and can dance, and I am sure he'll say yes."

Moments later, I was dialing his number, and shortly after that, he was eagerly agreeing to attend. Well, kind of.

"Sure, I'd love to go," he said. "But don't you think a Mardi Gras ball is …"

"Is what?" I asked.

"I mean, it's a weird first date, right? It's going to be loud and crowded. How about we get together before the ball?"

"Sure," I agreed, glad I'd at least secured a date for the evening.

"So," Michael said. "What're you up to tonight?"

I stalled, one part of me eager to see him and the other stubbornly refusing to be available so last minute. I came up with some excuse, and we agreed, instead, to meet after the new year on January 3, seven days before the ball.

We'll get into the details in a second, but let me just say we hit it off right away on that first date. There was a lot of talking, even more laughter, and just lots of fun. In many ways, that night set the tone for much more to come.

On January 11, the day after the ball and eight days after our first date, I called Melissa.

"Hey," she answered.

"You know what? I'm going to marry your friend Michael," I told her without preamble.

"Hold," she said. And suddenly the line went quiet. A moment later she was back. "Okay, now *what* did you say?"

"I said I'm going to marry Michael."

It wasn't until our engagement party four months later that I heard the rest of that story. Turns out Michael had been on the other line with Melissa.

He Said: The Date That Wasn't

Of the two of us, I'm the introvert. And Jaci's the opposite. She's the one always talking, bustling about, full of energy and life. She's the personality and face of our agency, and pretty much has been from the very beginning.

When we go out, Jaci's the one everyone knows. I'm usually greeted with a polite handshake and an, "Oh, you're Jaci's husband." Rarely the opposite. And to be honest, I am good with that, preferring to remain in the shadows until called upon to provide my own unique and brilliant perspective.

 **Jaci:** If you could only see my eyes rolling into the back of my head. The truth is, he remains in the shadows so no one will notice that he isn't wearing any shoes, but we'll come back to that later.

So, while Jaci was in LA, working with celebrities and making movies, I was still fighting my way through school, where I spent seven and a half years earning my degree. Yes, that's right. Seven and a half years. One degree. Same major. No time off.

It would be simple to say I enjoyed my collegiate experience a bit too much, but in all honesty, working my way through college while bartending at night caused some delays. Then of course there were the extracurriculars, like performing in musicals and my brief stint with the formation of the school's first-ever Italian American Student Federation Bocce team. (And no, I didn't make that up, it was a real thing.)

After my eventual graduation, I took my degree and trusty portfolio and headed to Seattle. Why Seattle? Well, it was the '90s, grunge was in, and the movie *Singles* had just come out, which made the Northwest look very appealing. Plus, a few friends of mine from college had moved there a few years prior, and it seemed to be the farthest place I could travel away from home. One of those friends was Melissa, who let me crash on her couch for a few weeks while I searched for work and a place of my own.

I remained in Seattle for several years, freelancing as a designer and copywriter by day and working at

Buca Di Beppo, a newly opened Italian restaurant, by night. It was Buca's fifth restaurant to open nationally, and in many ways, I learned more about branding and how important it was to form emotional connections with the consumer there than I did working in advertising. I learned things like the importance of knowing who you are as a brand, who your audience is, and how to form and deliver on your promise consistently through every touchpoint, from the way the hostess greets you at the door to the actual ambiance, including music, food, and even the bathrooms. I had no idea at the time, but my experiences working at Buca would later help define my philosophies on branding and how telling your story the right way can have a big impact.

Eventually the lack of sunlight and the nagging desire to leave the restaurant lifestyle behind and focus instead on my career took its toll. Plus, I was ready to try something new, even though I wasn't entirely sure what just yet.

While I was trying to figure it out, I moved back home to Louisiana and accepted a position as art director at a local agency. My plans were to save money and then take on the next great adventure. At the time, I had no clue that adventure would begin at a party I never wanted to attend in the first place.

Now, before I get into all of that, I need to make one thing perfectly clear: it was Jaci who chased me down as I was leaving the party, and I do mean chased. Some might even say she made a spectacle of herself the way she frantically called out for me.

Jaci: See? I told you we remember this differently.

In any event, I was pleased to hear from her a few days later and gladly accepted her invitation to attend the ball. To be honest, Jaci was everything I wasn't. An extrovert who carried herself with a level of confidence that few have. Sure, plenty of people pretend to have it all together, but with Jaci, you just believe it. It's what draws people to her and why it's so easy to trust in what she says. Now, I'm not putting all of this in writing because I'm foolish enough to think it'll earn me any brownie points or anything. God knows none of these statements is going to magically make my life any easier the next time a disagreement crops up and our office or home (or the grocery store, for that matter) turns into a quasi-battleground—again. But in all honesty, this attribute of Jaci's was one of the reasons I was looking forward to spending more time with her.

I suggested we meet before the holidays so we could get to know each other before the event. Unfortunately, she was busy, and it would have to wait until after New Year's. I say unfortunately because I already had plans with another girl on New Year's Eve and, well, long story short, I spent pretty much every penny I had that night trying to keep up with my more well-funded peers.

I can't even remember the name of my date, much less the night in general, other than by the time my date with Jaci rolled around, I was completely broke.

She Said: The Hunger Game

There are a couple of facts I should clear up. First, I didn't *chase* Michael. That's ridiculous.

Second, when we met, Michael was an artist and musician. He was also a painter and a writer, and he sang in an a cappella quartet that performed countrywide. He is vastly talented, this one. Unfortunately, none of these talents fell in the financial arena.

The Michael of then was one of those people who had full faith in the ATM, believing there was a magical genie that lived inside who knew exactly how much money he had. He hadn't quite grasped the concept of bounced checks or why people bothered balancing a checkbook, for that matter.

Comparatively, I was a little more settled and could very easily have said, "Oh, I got dinner. No problem." I wouldn't have thought twice about it. It wouldn't have been a big deal. And no, it wouldn't have changed the dynamics of our relationship, either. But the thing is, he'd *offered* to take *me* out, so I felt I was only following social protocol by letting him foot the bill.

But before we get to the fiasco that was our date at TGI Friday's, let me start at the beginning.

The night started well enough with Michael picking me up and asking where I wanted to go. For the life of me, I can't imagine what was going through his head. In hindsight, knowing he had no money, I'm baffled that he was still moving forward as if somehow things would just work out. I guess I should have seen the writing on the wall at this point, and yet, I still ended up marrying the guy.

But I digress. At my request, we stopped by a former sorority sister's wedding celebration on the way to dinner. To his credit, he rolled right along with everything.

Once we were done, we headed to a TGI Friday's at his suggestion. This would not have been my first choice, but I agreed because it was a place we could relax and talk without shouting over blaring music. The moment we were seated, I snatched up the menu, ready to eat.

When the waitress asked if we wanted to start with something, Michael asked if I wanted a soda. Not a beer. Not a glass of wine. A soda.

So we ordered sodas. Sip after sip I waited, my eyes gazing longingly at my discarded menu sitting dejectedly at the table's edge, hoping to hear the magic words "What would you like to order?" But that request never came.

Seriously. He never offered me anything. So, I sucked it up and tried to hide the grumbling of my stomach.

Eleven o'clock that night, before his car had a chance to clear my street, I jumped into my car, and in moments I was screeching into the drive-through of Taco Bell, where I ordered every damned item off the dollar menu.

He Said: And They Lived Snappily Ever After

So, here's the thing. No matter what she says, she still married me. And let me be the first to say I've paid for that night every single time we have gone out ever since. Jaci likes to browse the entire menu, glares at me, and jabs her finger at the most expensive item. Every time. And now so do my daughters, by the way. She's trained them well.

Oh, and Melissa? The night Jaci was on the phone with her and said she'd marry me? I was on the other line. And I'd basically told her the same thing. Today, Melissa's married to my best friend Kody, and they live here in Lafayette near us. Jaci and I set them up on their first date.

Our eventual marriage gave birth to many things that we are extremely proud of. Four kids in four years, yes, but also our agency, brandRUSSO, which we launched after our first child, Jackson, was born. We made our fair share of mistakes along the way, but over time we learned a lot about who we were, what we had to offer, and how we could translate that into a process that would benefit those we had the privilege of serving.

PART I: BRAND BEGINNINGS

CHAPTER 2: EQUAL PARTS CREATIVE AND STRATEGY

To be perfectly honest, opening our own shop was never part of the plan. At least not at first. Instead, we decided to jump right into parenthood. Around ten months after returning from our honeymoon, we welcomed Jackson into the world. Not long after, Jaci was pregnant with Jordan, and that's when we decided it was time to go out on our own. Well, sort of.

Jaci was the first to leap. She was a marketing strategist and media buyer at the time, and I was working at a regional ad agency. Looking back, I think it was something my dad said that led to us embracing such a risky endeavor. He said, "You will never get ahead collecting a W2." In fact, I believe he yelled it at Sunday dinner during one of his notorious tirades.

In retrospect, it was one of the best pieces of advice we ever received, and it completely changed our future.

 **Jaci:** Michael's dad was right, but more than that, I wanted more flexibility in not only our time, but also our future. I had traveled down the path of working eighteen-hour days and knew that would not fly with a growing family. I wanted to have the freedom to be a mom but also have a career doing what I loved. Plus, I knew that together, we had something to offer the world, even if at the time I wasn't sure exactly what that was.

Now, getting rich was never our goal, but having control over our lives, our time, and our future was. We wanted to create an environment where we ourselves would want to work—a place with no clock punching, micromanaging, or dress codes, a place to be strategic and creative without having to choose, a place to be serious about what we did without having our jobs define us.

And just like that, brandRUSSO was born.

She Said: And So It Began

Seriously, though? What the hell were we thinking? What was *I* thinking? Eight months pregnant with a one-and-a-half-year-old and I decide to leave my job to start a business. He never thought to tell me this may not have been the right time?

 Michael: If you haven't figured it out by now, Jaci isn't really the type of person you can convince of anything once she has her mind made up. So, no. I figured she had a plan and it would all work out over time. Thing is, there was no plan outside of just jumping in the deep end.

 **Jaci:** Well, there was and there wasn't. I knew we had the experience, talent, and drive to make it work. But more than that, I believed

that by combining strategy and creative we could provide something that was both unique and desired in the marketplace. We just had to figure out a process that made both of those disciplines work in harmony.

At the get-go, we were just a traditional ad agency doing the things every other agency did, like print, TV, radio, and collateral.

But our direction began to shift on a weekend trip to New Orleans. Like on most trips, we spent a fair amount of time dealing with work issues, coming to the realization that owning a business meant there really weren't any days off.

It was then that we began talking about the direction of our agency and how we could take the experience we gained working in larger markets and incorporate that at a local level. We both knew the world was changing and that the typical brochure, TV campaign, and print ads were no longer going to cut it. Instead, we had to find a better way to build loyalty and advocacy for our clients, and the only way to do that was to establish strong emotional connections.

Michael: We realized we were already incorporating most of these ideas into our work instinctively, but to go all in and change how we pursued clients and developed work for them would require a more detailed and executable process, both internally and externally.

The works of authors like Marty Neumeier, Seth Godin, and Al Ries were literary playbooks for me. They validated what we already knew—that branding was the answer.

Soon we began to change not only the way we talked about marketing and advertising, but also the way we approached each project, whether it was developing an identity system or an entire ad campaign. We knew we could no longer approach the deliverables without first considering the strategies behind them, and more importantly, the audiences they were intended for.

I mean, was providing the standard brochure and TV spot enough without first understanding—*truly* understanding—who it was we were trying to reach?

29

And with so many new online media channels cropping up and social media emerging, we could no longer depend on traditional methods of developing or delivering our clients' messaging.

This was the catalyst to us developing our own principles and a system of brand building from the inside out—a repeatable process that could be applied to any business or service, regardless of location, size, or industry.

Today, the word "branding" has become part of daily vernacular. Unfortunately, the term has been used and abused and become so commonplace that its essence is watered down, with many unsure of what it truly even means. Our goal was to provide some definitive reasoning and real-world explanations of what branding is and how it can be used to build business and increase consumer loyalty. But more on that a little later.

He Said: Front of the House, Back of the House

Jaci and I both come from restaurant backgrounds, having worked our way through college waiting tables and tending bar. We've learned a ton from those experiences, so much in fact that we often lean toward hiring people who have worked in the service industry. Generally, it shows that they are good with people, can read a room, can understand sales, can handle pressure, and are self-sufficient at managing their own tasks and responsibilities.

Our agency was also modeled, in part, on the same front-of-the-house and back-of-the-house mentalities used in restaurants. The idea was to give our back-of-the-house creatives (writers, designers, and programmers) the space and freedom to work without distraction and disruption, while the front of the house (brand developers, strategists, and sales) shouldered more direct client interaction. Originally, we did this to maintain some distance between Jaci and me (a key to surviving a work/spouse relationship), but we soon found that it also helped to streamline our workflow and improve productivity and communication.

Internally, however, the lines between strategy and creative often blurred, with both sides playing a vital part in the final outcome of every project. This was by design, helping to incorporate the strengths Jaci and I both bring to the table. It's also the foundation of our process and what makes branding such a powerful marketing tool when both disciplines are applied.

A good example of how this works looks a lot like your typical night out at a restaurant. Generally, you never see the chef at work, with the host and waitstaff handling the customer service. They remain out front, reading each table as they help guide the overall guest experience. But when called upon, the chef will leave the line, put on his pressed white chef's coat, and make an appearance on the dining room floor. Similarly, our entire creative team remains in the "back of the house" until we are called into a new client meeting with an understanding that the "meal" we're preparing is always going to be better if we have a good sense of who we're preparing it for.

In these cases, I'll slide on my good shoes from my shoe collection beneath my desk and join in the conversation.

Once we've met with the client and gathered the information needed, we disappear again until it's time to present our final work, leaving the additional gathering of research to our assigned research teams.

Jaci: Literally, he's not kidding. When I walk clients through the agency, I'm like, "Hey, Michael. I have a client out front. Can you put your shoes on and come meet them, please?" Oh, and when he says "good shoes," he means his good pair of Crocs.

At brandRUSSO, Jaci drives the train, serving as lead strategist and CEO, and I head up the creative team. Division of labor at its best. And while most would say you can't have two bosses, just like you can't have two chefs in the kitchen, our process works best with the checks and balances that come from an equal partnership of strategy and creative combined.

For the most part, this strategy has worked well for the growth of our agency and the growth of our clients, and that has always been our driving force: making sure that the work we do for our clients produces results. Sure, there are no guarantees in advertising, but we believe that when you follow a proven process backed by consumer insight and creative that is led by strategy, the potential for success is always high.

For us, it has never been about awards or putting the spotlight on ourselves, but rather, always ensuring that our clients get the attention they deserve.

Jaci: When we bought our current building and remodeled it in 2006, we installed three shelves for awards in our conference room. Once they were filled, we stopped entering contests altogether. I know this is going to sound cliché, but we learned early on that the only rewards that really matter are the ones that come from producing results for our clients.

BUT WHAT MAKES US SO CERTAIN OF OUR WORTH WITHOUT CONSTANT VALIDATION FROM ANYONE OTHER THAN CLIENTS?

It comes from the knowledge that our process works, regardless of size, industry, or location. It's a process that, when followed, provides the best chances for success. But before we can begin talking about that process, we have to first establish our definition of branding, along with the principles that support it.

CHAPTER 3: SO, WHAT IS A BRAND?

At first glance, it sounds like a silly question. After all, the term branding has become part of our everyday vernacular. But with so many interpretations and uses, it's important to bring some clarity to what it means for practical usage.

But before we talk about what a brand is, let's talk about what it is not.

TO BEGIN WITH, A BRAND IS NOT A LOGO. I REPEAT. A BRAND IS NOT A LOGO.

Don't get me wrong, we love logos. They are a crucial piece of any branding process and vital in properly representing any business or organization, but a logo alone is not a brand in and of itself.

And no, it's not a company, product, service, or personality either, regardless of how many celebrities or sports stars refer to themselves as one.

ON THE CONTRARY:

A brand is a person's emotional connection with a company, product, or service.

– Marty Neumeier

The two most important words in that definition are "emotional connection." That's where the magic happens, and that's where great brands are born.

She Said: The B-Word

Whether you're checking out your friend's shoes, talking smartphones, or discussing your favorite clothing line, you're likely to utter the B-word at some point (branding, of course). It's tossed around so freely that now it means just about everything under the sun—and therefore nothing at all. There's so much ambiguity and confusion about what branding actually even is. Marty Neumeier, one of my favorites, makes this point very well in his book *The Brand Gap*. His definition of a brand is "your gut reaction to something." I couldn't agree more. I just wish I'd said it first.

Take, for example, the upward swoosh of the Nike logo or the Medusa-like hair on your Starbucks cup—those aren't brands. They're logos, or a brand's identity. Kind of like how humans have faces that help us tell each other apart, brands have logos that let us spot them in a crowd. But a logo on its own isn't branding.

Like Michael said, branding is the emotional connection your product, company, or service evokes within your customer. An emotional connection doesn't happen in your mind. It happens in your heart, which is why I always say, "the brand is in the heart of the beholder."

But here's the catch: no matter how incredible a job you think you've done creating that heartfelt emotional connection, it's only as real as your audience perceives. If your customer doesn't *feel* your brand, you might as well not have one.

He Said: Don't Get Mixed by Emotions

Usually when people hear "emotional connection" they get confused, immediately thinking of a sad, tugging-on-your-heartstrings kind of experience. But that's not what we're talking about here. In truth, we're talking about forming emotional connections, not just causing them. Sure, touching someone in a way that inspires emotions is never a bad thing, whether it elicits laughter or tears. But when it comes to branding, these emotions often end up wasted if they don't properly link back to the brand.

When we talk about forming emotional connections, which we do often, we're referring to what consumers feel about a product, company, or service and why they choose them over the competition. What makes them loyal? What helps them develop ownership? What makes them want to join *that* company's tribe?

Imagine yourself in the peanut butter aisle of your grocery store with shelves and shelves of peanut butter jars stretching out before you. You stand there for what seems like an eternity considering all of the options. Then, in a moment of decisiveness, you reach for "the chosen one." The one that seems to be calling your name, making you wonder if anyone else around you can hear that container of nut butter actually talking. You're happy with your choice and like the way it makes you feel. But what was it that *caused* that feeling? After all, it's just a jar of peanut butter.

Does its taste remind you of the PB&Js your mom used to make you, crusts carefully cut off? Or possibly those 3 a.m. nights at your college dorm when that was all you had to eat? Does it bring you joy or make you nostalgic for simpler times?

THAT, MY FRIENDS, IS AN EMOTIONAL CONNECTION.

The important thing to remember is that this connection has nothing to do with peanut butter and everything to do with the story behind it. The question is, how do you tell your story in a way that evokes the same type of response?

Truth is, there are many ways to form emotional connections with your audience. Sometimes it's through deep, heartfelt stories. Sometimes it's by getting you to laugh or making you cry. Sometimes it can be through science. Sometimes it's through personal experience and relatability. And sometimes, it's because your story is just better than everyone else's on the shelf.

She Said: Why Brand?

So, we're finally at this question about branding, and I'm going to paint you a picture, because that's always more fun.

Say you own a local restaurant with a claim that you serve the absolute best burgers in town. When Consumer A walks in, they're expecting to get the absolute best burger, because, well, you know, you promised it. You then proceed to deliver on that promise by doing exactly what you said you would. Consumer A is now a believer in your promise and your brand, and chances are, they're going to come back, because they trust you will provide the same experience each time.

And then here comes the cool part—as a soon-to-be-loyal patron and new member of your tribe, Consumer A starts raving about you. He's tweeting about your restaurant, bringing his coworkers over for lunch, and swinging by on the weekends with family. Consumer A has ownership now. He's transformed into a walking, talking advocate. He's putting his name behind yours on social media, the largest megaphone in the marketing industry. But he's also placing his credibility and reputation on the line, because in representing you, he's also representing himself. And this type of advocacy is the clear goal in branding, because it leads to word-of-mouth marketing, which creates the best ROI any business could hope for.

So now let's put it in words: why is branding important? Because a brand helps shape your personality and identity. It tells people who you are. And if you're not the one telling them what they should feel or think about you—and then proving it—they'll make their own assumptions, which might not always work in your favor. So better to tell your story and prove it by making and then delivering on your promise at all times. And that's exactly what branding does—it shifts the narrative in your favor.

He Said: Debunking the Myth

As we'll cover in more detail when we talk about the 5 Rs, many companies naïvely think they own their brands. After all, they're the ones writing checks to push their message out to the public, whether it's through TV, radio, or print. These channels offer one-way monologues with the company doing all the talking. So it only makes sense that they control how they're perceived, right? Hmm, no. That changed around … oh, the time Mark Zuckerberg invented Facebook. Now people have the power to talk back and kick monologues out the door.

Consumers have the power to share their opinions on posts, praise businesses that do things right, and bitch about those that don't. And nowadays it's *consumers* who do most of the talking—long after companies have stopped.

This power shift makes you subservient to customers' wants, needs, and impressions. It means you have to build relationships. That's where branding comes in.

And while you can't dictate what your audience might think of you, you can help influence their decisions. You accomplish this by creating messages that resonate and inspire – clearly communicating how what you provide can enhance their lives in some way.

She Said: How Does Branding Really Work?

Branding, much like our marriage, is about duality. Michael and I are husband and wife. We're business partners. One's captain of the home and the other's captain of the ship. Basically, we're opposite faces of the same coin.

AND BRANDING—LIKE US—HAS THE SAME DUALITY, TWO EQUAL PARTS: STRATEGY AND CREATIVE.

Let's talk about what that means for a second. Yes, it's so cool to have a beautiful, well-designed corporate brochure with striking colors and high end photography. Maybe you've even had it printed on paper handwoven by Himalayan monks. But do any of those things really matter? The point of branding is to help cut through the clutter, not add to it.

Does that handwoven paper help you truly stand out? Or does that process take you away from the most important element—the message?

Of course, the quality of design and materials matters. But if there is no substance behind what your putting out there, then it might as well be just another pretty piece of art. And if there is no strategy behind the development of the piece itself outside of being really cool, then chances are it won't be too long before that piece of art is lining a wastebasket.

Being married to a creative makes what I am about to say tough (even though he knows it's true)—but creativity without strategy is a brand killer. In many ways, it promotes false advertising, promising something more than what the company, product, or service actually delivers and going against the promise behind the brand. This type of window dressing fails to prove the authenticity that today's consumers demand, and while you can get away with it for some time—just like all new, shiny, pretty things do—in time, clients will want more.

I'm all about creativity. But we never let creative lead strategy.

Instead, we do our best to find harmony between the two, letting each side of the coin have its say on the way to finding the best possible solution.

Michael: In the entrance to our building, we have a quote from Jef Richards that I think aptly describes what Jaci is trying to articulate— "Creative without strategy is art. Creative with strategy is advertising." I came across this quote while I was touring agencies in Texas back in college. I like to think if Jef had written that today, it would have said, "Creative with strategy is branding."

Take Superbowl ads as an example. A company could create the most amazing, knee-slappingly hilarious ad, but if it doesn't move the needle and inspire some form of consumer behavior, all the creativity in the world won't make a difference.

So, before you sign on for the Himalayan handwoven paper, ask yourself if it will improve your bottom line. Ultimately, it's your message that drives the sales or phone calls or whatever action it is you want your customers to take.

PART II: THE RUSSO WAY

CHAPTER 4: THE 5 RS

First Bank and Trust, one of our first large clients, was known as the official bank of the New Orleans Saints football team. Just claiming that title cost them about ninety percent of their marketing budget. That wasn't the greatest news for us, because it meant that when they hired us to create value for that sponsorship, they had only ten percent of the budget remaining to spend on actual marketing.

Regardless, we got to work, comparing the messaging of competitor banks and trying to figure out a unique way to position First Bank and Trust. Before we could resolve their positioning, we had to first discover who it was they were talking to.

After some research, we learned that First Bank and Trust had a reputation of working with small- to medium-sized businesses post-Hurricane Katrina, helping countless businesses rebuild following the widespread disaster. With several other key research findings, we decided to position them as a business-first financial institution, along with the eventual tagline: "Business. Made Personal."

In order to support this initiative while also utilizing the equity gained from the Saints sponsorship, we set out to invent a fictional character that helped to bridge both worlds.

MEET FIRST BANK FRED.

"Fred is a self-proclaimed ultimate Saints fan. What makes Fred an ultimate Saints fan?

"Well, for starters, Fred thought it would be a great idea to name all of his children after his favorite Saints players. Little Hokie, Deuce, Dalton, Ricky, Reggie, Willie, and his baby girl Archie remind him daily of his love for everything Saints.

"Fred drives a black and gold car, lives in a black and gold house, and most recently, made the move to First Bank and Trust, the Official Banking Partner of the New Orleans Saints.

"Let your black and gold colors fly and become

an ultimate Saints fan just like Fred—naming your firstborn after your favorite Saints player is completely optional."

Our first step was to find a suitable Fred who could attend games, be easily recognized, be featured in print ads, promote bank events, and pretty much be everywhere at once. This would have been a difficult task even with an unlimited budget, but since our hands were tied with limited means we decided to build a Fred persona that could be easily replicated without breaking the bank.

The end result was a suit-wearing businessman who wore an official Saints football helmet at all times and never spoke. This allowed different actors to play the role in a variety of situations.

A few weeks into the campaign, Fred became a folk hero. People wanted to be near him, hang out with him, and take pictures with him. This took place at a time when social media was still in its infancy, providing an effective guerrilla and online marketing technique.

For Saints home games, Fred would lead a second line with a live marching band from the bank to the Superdome, which was just down the street.

In the Superdome, a professional photographer followed Fred, snapping pictures of him with fans. After each picture, Fred would extract a business card from his lanyard, with a link to the site where the photos would later be loaded for people to view and save.

First Bank Fred was effective in leveraging the money spent on the Saints sponsorship, as well as beginning the process of branding the bank as a friend to the business community. To build on this, we decided to take advantage of the resources that came with the sponsorship.

In this second leg of this campaign, we utilized the Superdome suite that came with the sponsorship to perform a business "matchmaking" service between top current clients from each category of industry and prospective clients the bank desired. We'd introduce these businesses to each other right before games, creating small ecosystems where they could network among themselves and conduct business deals while enjoying an event on the bank's dime.

Later, they'd even get a chance to snap a picture

with First Bank Fred, who always made a timely appearance. With an understanding that current clients were and are the best word-of-mouth marketers to prospective clients, we made sure to have plenty of both on hand at each game, which led to an avalanche of new business opportunities.

Of course, there was a caveat. Football season only lasted so long. How would we keep the momentum going once it was over? We couldn't pimp Fred out to a baseball game. After all, he was a Saints guy.

The third leg of the campaign—called *What Next?*—addressed this, focusing on young entrepreneurs, established community leaders, and growing businesses that were ready to transition to the next phase of their business lives. We targeted people who were expanding their offerings, opening new locations, or launching new services and products, demonstrating how the bank could help propel them in their journey. The *What Next?* campaign enabled us to keep connecting with customers in the off season until football season rolled around again.

When all was said and done, we helped leverage the bank's position as the "Official Bank of the New Orleans Saints" while positioning them as a trusted business partner throughout the Gulf South. Along the way, we helped unify the bank's brand standards in preparation for continued growth and increased acquisitions.

Following the launch and implementation of the campaign, the bank had a 22 percent growth of assets—which was even more remarkable considering the region was still recovering from Hurricane Katrina.

But how did we do so much with so little? Was it luck, or did we go in knowing that our recommendations and deliverables were going to work? And what helped guide us toward these solutions? What was the process behind our thoughts, and how did we manage to make it all come together?

For us, it always begins with the 5 Rs: realize, resolve, reinvent, relate, and react.

These branding principles serve as the core foundations of our process, laying a roadmap for everything that follows. They also break down the confusion and misunderstandings surrounding what branding actually is.

We will get into answering that question a little later, but first, the 5 Rs.

With an understanding that many of the clients and marketing heads we worked with often had their own unique perceptions and understanding of branding, we knew we had to find a way to convey the *why* in addition to the *how*. And if we wanted to gain their trust, we had to not only explain our process better, but do it in a way that didn't require a doctorate in marketing to understand—and that's exactly what the five Rs do.

IT STARTS WITH REALIZATION

He Said: #1 Realize

REALIZE: THE CONSUMER OWNS THE BRAND

Your brand is defined by an emotional connection between you and your audience. While you can help influence their perceptions, you cannot dictate how they truly feel.

A national organization we were working with hired a reputable digital agency to manage their online ads. The agency handles basically everything for this client from an advertising perspective, from creating Google ads to finding the right search words and key terms to monitoring the performance of each campaign—

everything this client lives and dies by to boost their search engine placement.

Of course, getting your name at the top of the list is important—until it's not.

Wait, but if I'm one of the top-ranked sites, doesn't that mean more clicks—and more money? you might ask.

Well, possibly. But just because you're one of the first results on Google doesn't mean you've eliminated the competition. Truth is, buyers don't just click the first result; they weigh all the options on that first page, including competitors that likely offer the same service and products as you. So, why should/would they choose you?

Usually, the only way to stand apart at this point is through pricing, which often leads to a bidding war and the realization that your product or service has now become a commodity. That's when you're really screwed. Commoditization makes it hard to be a successful, profitable company, because now your value lies in outpricing competitors, which chips away at your profit margins and undermines the overall value of your brand.

Branding is the exact opposite of commoditization. The scenario we've just described is the perfect example of why branding is so integral—because it addresses why you're different, what your value is, and what makes you distinct beyond pricing.

By realizing and accepting that the consumer owns the brand, you are acknowledging that they are in control of how you're perceived and valued based on their experience prior, during, and after purchase.

In order to help influence these perceptions, we recommend asking the following questions:

- What "mental real estate" is yours to own?

- What emotions do you evoke?

- What differences can you authentically claim?

- Why should your audience care?

 **Jaci:** Discovering what makes you special helps your audience better understand how what you provide can enhance their lives. At the end

of the day, there will always be several names at the top of any list, and without the emotional connections that come from branding, there will be no reason for customers to choose you, unless it's because you were the cheapest. This may bring you some short-term gains, but no long-term rewards.

Takeaway: Realize that while you can help influence consumers' perceptions, they will ultimately come to their own conclusions based on their experiences and interactions with your brand.

She Said: #2 Resolve

RESOLVE: YOUR PROMISE IS YOUR BRAND

Your promise connects you to your audience, establishing the one thing that sets you apart from the competition—the assurance that it's a promise that can always be delivered.

Sometimes, to stand out from the pack and be heard above the noise, you have to change the conversation from what's already being said. By changing the conversation, you're able to clearly define your promise. In doing so, your audience can better understand how your offering can enhance their lives.

Remember the PC versus Mac ad on TV? The Mac guy was this cool graphic designer dude who dressed all hip. And the PC guy wore a suit and tie and nerdy glasses and slicked his hair down, like Dwight from *The Office*. As a laptop user, you're automatically part of one group or the other. And the statement the ad makes is bold: If you're a Mac, you're cool and hip. Meanwhile, PCs are snoring-boring.

Basically, Mac is saying: Hey, everybody who looks like this or sounds like this—or wants to be this—come on over. We got you. We're your people. This is brilliant because, as humans, we gravitate not only toward people who are like us, but often toward people that we feel best represent us.

In order to establish that one thing that sets you apart, you must find ways to be different, authentic, and change the conversation.

Truth is, people don't do business with businesses; they do business with *people*. That's why being authentic is so important. Authenticity can only come when you have a good understanding of who you are.

Once you know that, along with who it is you're trying to reach, you can easily define your promise, and your promise means everything. It's the unspoken contract with your audience that ensures expectations are met at all times. This leads to trust, loyalty, and advocacy, something that can only be earned.

Michael: The term "promise" is in no way a legally binding proposition, but rather, a single point of differentiation that can be authentically claimed and delivered on a consistent basis. It's your niche! And it is, in effect, the essence of the brand itself. We will cover the question of "What is a brand?" a little later, but for us, none of that matters without first establishing your promise.

Takeaway: To establish trust with your audience that also promotes ownership in your brand, you have to define your promise, then deliver it consistently across all of the touchpoints that your audience comes in contact with.

He Said: #3 Reinvent

REINVENT YOUR AUDIENCE IS IN CONTROL

Your audience is more in control of the information and communication they receive than ever before, and it is your responsibility to find ways to change with them. If not, you will soon find that you're yelling at an audience that can no longer hear the sound of your voice.

To combat this, you must make an effort to engage your audience through social media and other non-traditional media channels. You can have an amazing message, but if your audience never hears it, then you're wasting more than just your time.

Not all media channels are the same.

Kids in high school and college don't use the same social media channels as their parents. Instead, they continue to find their own unique spaces to live and communicate. What does that mean for marketers? It means they now have to reach their audience where they are—in all these different media channels, delivered in all these different ways. In other words, what worked yesterday probably won't work the same today.

By acknowledging this shift and reinventing how you approach your messaging, you open up new opportunities to connect with your target audience where they live, work, and play.

This may sound similar to the concept of the first R, realize—acknowledging that your audience is in control and driving the conversation. But I think the reinforcement is necessary, because I can't tell you how many companies still use the same dated tactics from years ago that just won't fly anymore. And it's one thing to simply realize these things, but it's another to reinvent how you react.

Just watch a local car dealership commercial and

you'll see what I mean. Chances are they'll spend airtime pricing products, screaming bargains, and yelling the same message repeatedly. That doesn't cut it anymore. Screaming at your audience and yelling prices isn't effective, and it doesn't help you build relationships with customers. In failing to reinvent themselves and adapt to changing times, these companies will end up spending much more to even hope that their message is heard.

Think back to the old way of marketing and advertising and you'll see it was that simple. All you had to do was buy a TV, radio, or print ad and broadcast your message there. That's how the majority of consumers would learn about you.

But today, we're operating in a different setting, with people focusing more on brand conversations where they happen the most—in front of hundreds of thousands of people on public platforms.

And where companies used to have complete control over their message, they're not even invited to the conversation anymore. Influencers as young as five determine the fate of brand-new products before they even have a chance to settle on retail store shelves.

CHAPTER 4: THE 5 RS

Jaci: This brings us back to promise. What promise are you making? Are you delivering on it? Are you building trust and loyalty? Because the people who are carrying on all these conversations are advocating for or against you, or they don't even care if you exist.

When you take time to reinvent yourself and build on your promise, you're setting the odds in your favor.

REMEMBER:

- You can't buy attention.
- You must be willing to listen.
- You have to be where your audience is.

Takeaway: Make a commitment to reinvent how you approach your marketing, messaging, and media channels to reach your audience.

She Said: #4 Relate

RELATE
DEVELOP A MESSAGING THAT
RESONATES

Everyone claims that their service is superior and that their customers are treated like friends. But far too often we treat our customers like unintelligent fools. We give them worn out messages tied to outdated delivery systems—ignoring their needs to force our agendas upon them.

Truth is, your customers want a brand they can believe in and feel connected to. Relate to your audience by discovering their wants and needs, then delivering on them, always creating content focused around the characteristics of your ideal customer.

Buying a car twenty years ago meant you were

at the mercy of a salesperson to shoot it straight and quote you the "best" deal. Today, before I even walk the lot, I know how much it costs to make a car, how much the dealer has in it, how long it's been on the lot, and what interest rate is being paid. Even better, I have an idea of exactly how desperate that dealer is to move that car. And when he says, "Sorry, ma'am, but we don't have that color," I know whether he's BSing me or not, because I have access to every dealer's inventory at the touch of my fingers.

Unlike before, the salesperson doesn't get to dictate how the sale is going to work. *I* know how it's going to work, because I have more information at my disposal than ever before. That's the customer of today. The moment they consider a product or choose a restaurant, the first thing they do is go online, read reviews, gather information, and research. What businesses are encountering today are the most informed consumers in the history of the world.

Consumers are too smart for fake promises and grand gestures, and to relate to them in a way that is authentic and real, you must be able to:

- speak their language,

- understand their needs, and
- treat them with respect.

 **Michael:** Think in terms of human-to-human connections. When two people can relate to one another, they gain a sense of belonging, becoming a part of something bigger than themselves. Relatability is what makes way for relationships. So when you're able to connect with your audience on an emotional level, you make it possible for your business to form long-lasting relationships with your consumers.

Takeaway: Without a clear understanding of who it is you're trying to reach, you're just hoping for the best—and hoping rarely ends well when it comes to advertising. Instead, get to know your audience and find ways to connect with them on an emotional level.

He Said: #5 React

REACT
GIVE THEM A
REASON TO
BELIEVE

No matter how creative your marketing is, a poorly positioned product, service, or brand will fail sooner or later. For this reason, you must develop what is most worthwhile to communicate—a reason for your audience to join your tribe.

Reacting is all about developing messaging that will resonate with your target audience. It's also about getting your ducks in a row to make sure people react to you the right way—the way you want.

It's also about having a professional logo, a name

you can trademark and call your own, profession-ally designed sales materials, and a great website and online presence—all of which ultimately promote a promising reaction from your audience.

In other words, don't get your secretary's brother's sister-in-law to create your branding materials for you (unless, of course, she's a pro). Don't cheap out on something so critical—something that reflects and represents who you are as a business and how you wish to be viewed by those you serve.

Unfortunately, messaging is often the last thing most companies take into consideration. It's an after-thought when compared to media buys, impressions, and click throughs. But without a message that tells your story—giving your audience the opportunity to connect on an emotional level—you might as well be speaking a different language.

When you walk the walk, and talk the talk, your audience will find you, be-cause:

- They want to have a sense of belonging and be part of something.

- They want to connect with others who are like them.

- They want to be in "the club."

Takeaway: Develop a relationship with your audience and always deliver on your difference. In doing so, you provide an opportunity for them to join your tribe and have an ownership in your success. People instinctively join tribes to become part of a community, so make sure you're providing a reason for them to believe.

She Said: Cleaning House

So, there you have the 5 Rs. We created them so we could formulate and organize our own beliefs and branding philosophies, as well as provide a resource for our clients to better understand why branding is so integral.

When you understand your audience and what motivates them, you can better understand how to connect with them. And make no mistake, connection is key. Sure, you can buy your way in, but chances are you wouldn't even need advertising if you had that kind of money to burn.

Now that we've covered that, let's talk about getting your house in order.

Fair warning: getting your house in order can be a painful process, requiring you to take a good, hard look in the mirror. It starts with your logo, your identity system, and your collateral, as well as your online presence, website, and messaging. Do all of these elements represent you properly? Do they tell your story when you aren't there to tell it yourself?

Here is where the 5 Rs begin to earn their keep, ensuring that every one of the touchpoints your audience interacts with properly reflects the promise behind your brand.

But how do you know when it's time to send out invitations?

Good question. Let's do a quick time travel through the history of advertising so you can get a better understanding of what our current landscape requires.

History of Advertising[1]

1900 Features – What it is

1925 Benefits – What it does for me

1950 Experience – How it makes me feel

2000 Belonging – Who I am

2010 Social – Who we are

In the early 1900s, advertising was all about highlighting the features of a product. Let's say you were a soap manufacturer. During this era, you'd focus on the features of your soap, so your ad might go something like this: *I make soap. Soap cleans your body. You need soap. Buy my soap.*

Fast forward to the 1920s, and we'd moved on from features to benefits. Because now, all of a sudden, there were several soap manufacturers to choose from, so the only way to break above the noise was to distinguish why your soap was superior to the next: *My soap is made with natural ingredients—so it won't harm your skin, unlike the competitor's.*

By the time the 1950s rolled around, World

---

1   Marty Neumeier, *The Brand Gap* (Indianapolis, Indiana: New Riders, 2003).

War II had ended, and people had more money to work with. Families were moving to the suburbs and purchasing homes with sprawling backyards. To differentiate products, the focus of marketing became all about living your best life and having good experiences. The buzz question, then, became: *How does this make me feel?*

Advertising, in turn, shifted to this type of messaging: *If you buy my product, you will feel better about yourself. People will like you more.*

In the 2000s, features and benefits were no longer enough. Now it's about identity, making people feel like they belong, and creating a connection. And perhaps most importantly, this is when social media began to steal the spotlight, and for good reason.

Today, that's where your audience lives, works, and plays—and it's where the majority of the conversations about and by you will take place. And while social media is one of the most powerful resources for connecting with people, forming relationships, and building a tribe of loyal followers, that doesn't mean traditional media doesn't have a seat at the table. Quite the opposite, actually. To use it effectively, however, you have to understand your audience and how to best reach them—ensuring your message touches them at multiple moments in their lives.

Michael: Your message must be delivered everywhere your audience comes into contact with your brand. If the experience as a whole doesn't support your promise, the brand will either suffer or, at best, fail to build loyalty and advocacy. In the end, one can't live without the other, and each depends heavily on the other to be successful.

CHAPTER 5: WHAT'S IN A MESSAGE? WELL, EVERYTHING

So far, we've covered how crucial it is to define your promise, understand your audience, and utilize strategy when it comes to branding. One without the other could affect how you're perceived and, in the end, how successful you are. While it's fair to say that you can get by with strong messaging alone, you cannot create a strong message without first developing and understanding your promise, audience, and strategy. And to be very clear, messaging is an essential part of forming these emotional connections we keep mentioning.

Remember, you have to first know your audience before you can even hope to form emotional connections and, in turn, develop messaging that will help influence their perceptions.

For many, this would begin with gathering demographics.

Marketing 101 has always taught us that demographics are the magic potion for advertising success. However, demographics alone aren't the answer anymore. Yes, they still play a part, but in no way are they the go-to they once were. Today, your audience is much more dynamic, and categorizing people based on age, race, or gender rarely tells the whole story. That's why we use something called psychographic profiling.

A good example of effective psychographic profiling can best be illustrated through our work for a radio station that hired us to help them rebrand. Its marketing team came armed with folders full of stats and numbers. "Alright," they said. "We've hired a market researcher who determined that our typical demographic of listeners is college-educated women between the ages of twenty-five and fifty-four with two to four kids." And sure, they were right. Kind of.

Jaci: Using standard demographic profiles, media buyers often place women into buckets. For example, women ages twenty-five to fifty-four is a demographic bucket, but if you looked closer, you would realize that the twenty-five-year-old women and the fifty-four-year-old women actually have very little in common.

Twenty-five-year-old women, generally, are just emerging from college, starting a job, and beginning a serious relationship that could lead to marriage and a new family. Fifty-four-year-old women, on the other hand, are at the peak of their income potential with established careers. They've either already been married for some time, moved on to another relationship or second marriage, are soon-to-be empty nesters, or are becoming grandmothers. Both populations of women probably watch *Grey's Anatomy*, but for certain they don't watch it the same way.

The fifty-four-year-old is probably watching it

live Thursday night while the twenty-five-year-old is likely powering on Netflix or Hulu to binge watch the five seasons she never even knew existed.

To add to that, the demographics that considered only age did not properly capture the differences in the way these two groups viewed themselves. Many of the women that fell into the older demographic were having children much later in life and did not consider themselves to be "old." On the contrary, they were more active and involved than their parents were at that age, and remained plugged in to current trends in fashion, lifestyle choices—and yes, music, too.

Once we knew more about who these women were, we were able to help the radio station revamp both its programming and messaging. Using demographics alone, we would never have uncovered pertinent details about them and would have most likely missed the mark on connecting with them on an emotional level. But examining the audience's psychographic profile made us realize that women in this demographic were behaving outside the expected norm, enabling us to develop messaging that included them in the conversation and showcased how what the client was offering could benefit their lives.

She Said: Personality Means Everything

At our agency, we use personality profiles to help us identify who it is we're talking to. These profiles help us gain the insight needed to create the type of messaging that will resonate and motivate consumer behavior. One of the ways we approach this is derived from Stuart Sanders and his take on the four personality types that every brand must take into consideration. To me, it's a lot like the five love languages—working to identify how to talk to people in the language they best understand.

For example, traditional print ads are made up of four basic quadrants: a headline, body copy, an image/illustration, and a logo. Sanders took each of these quadrants and translated them into the four unique personality types, giving us a way to ensure the messaging we develop speaks directly to the target audience. I first learned this device in the '90s, and at its core, it remains relevant even today.

He Said: The Headline

The Headline is just like it sounds—the person who skims only the headlines of an article. They're not your read-every-word-on-the-page kind of person. Instead, the Headline prefers to glance through the bullet points and pull-out quotes, their eyes swiftly drifting to the quick-read summaries of blog posts. They're usually the big-picture, quick-vision type who trust their gut instinct, make a speedy decision, and stick to it. If it doesn't work out, fine. They pivot and do it a different way. They're not the type to lose time or sleep worrying about the details.

I know a little bit about Headlines, not because I am one, but because I'm married to one. At first thought, you might believe having a headline personality type for a business partner is a great thing. I mean, who wouldn't want their CEO to be fast-moving, fast-talking, and able to calmly navigate troubled waters without breaking a sweat? But I assure you, there are challenges as well. Like, when she decides to "skim" through the copy I spent three weeks working on during a client presentation.

She Said: The Body Copy

The Body Copy is the exact opposite of The Headline and is all about the details. They want as much specific information as possible, and when they're finished reading said information, they go somewhere else to read even more. Body Copies are equal opportunity investigators, spending countless hours researching websites, case studies, and everything else they can get their clutches on. They have questions about their list of questions. For them, it's all about the details. Sometimes this can lend itself to a little analysis paralysis. I know, because Michael is a casebook Body Copy. Want an example? I think I can cover that.

Pretty much anytime we decide to go out to dinner, the conversation usually starts around lunchtime, with Michael asking where we should eat. Fast forward to five hours later when we're pulling into the parking lot of the restaurant, and he's still considering options. Seriously? Why are we still talking about where else to go when we are already sitting down to actually eat?

So, for these special types of people, you have to make sure they have plenty of information that they can use to absorb. If not, you'll lose their trust, or they'll suspect you're being shady or hiding something. You can avoid this by giving them plenty of options to consider.

He Said: The Illustration

The Illustration is all about the pretty pictures. They skip the headlines and the copy and go right to the visuals. Probably the most interesting fact about this personality type is its fixation on the "me." It's not uncommon for The Illustration to get caught up with questions and thoughts like "How does this make *me* feel? How does this make *me* look?"

I need to make sure that this product/service puts *me* in a positive light.

The Illustration is all about being the first to adopt a product and is also a sucker for being part of the best that's out there, because they see themselves as a reflection of that superiority. And of course, Illustrations love awards, since they serve as validation of that superiority.

To be blunt, The Illustration is all about looking good. They're going to drive a car that makes them look good—making sure they toss their BMW key fob on the bar for everyone to see. They're also early adopters of technology, ensuring that they have the latest and the greatest before anyone else.

It's important to remember that when developing personality profiles, you have to always consider the outliers. You know, the ones that never fit into one category.

Take Jaci, for example. While she is clearly a Headline, she can be a bit of an Illustration as well. I know this because of two things: 1) She drives a Tesla, and we all know the first rule of owning a Tesla—tell everyone you meet that you own a Tesla. 2) There is not a piece of technology this woman does not own.

She Said: The Logo

Where The Illustration is about the "me," The Logo is about the "we."

How do we feel?
How are we going to handle this?

Companies that care about the community, environment, and giving back appeal to The Logo. But at the same time, The Logo is perfectly fine sitting back, waiting, and watching to make sure others have strong, risk-free experiences with a company before they themselves jump in feet-first.

They also seek companies that have interests and concerns similar to their own and enjoy doing business with those who care about people like them. If a company meets all of these criteria, The Logo's all in.

And if the company continues to meet or exceed The Logo's expectations over time, you can bet they've secured a customer for life. Because losing a Logo is a lot like losing a car in your garage.

Logos are also about collaboration and peer groups and can often be found on Facebook saying, "I need a new (fill in the blank here)." Then they'll wait for the responses to trickle in before they decide where to go. Logos want to know what's already been endorsed and rely on the opinions of peer group or online reviews to help them make decisions. Testimonials are also crucial to Logos.

While it might be tempting to force each person into one specific group, chances are most people will fall into several categories. For example, Michael is a bit of a Logo and an Illustration, and I am a whole lot of Headline with just a bit of Illustration.

In addition, you could easily compare these four different personality types to their DiSC profile counterparts.

Trust me, I've never met a BuzzFeed questionnaire or *Cosmo* personality test I didn't like.

I love these kinds of things, and if you look at the DiSC profile system, you'll see they're closely aligned with the four personality types we just described. The headlines are the D's, Illustrations are the I's, Body Copies are the S's, and Logos are the C's.

As I mentioned earlier, these personality types remind me of the Five Love Languages. What it really comes down to is talking to people in the language they best understand, because in the end, we do business with people we like—and we need to know that people understand us and speak our language. That's the whole point of the Five Love Languages; they describe the different ways people show and receive love. The same is true with marketing. If you want to reach a Headline, you have to put out Headline bait. If you want to reach a Body Copy, you have to put out Body Copy materials.

Ultimately, knowing the type of personality profiles you're dealing with can lend greater focus to your message, helping you ensure you're using the most impactful messaging approach.

CHAPTER 6: RAZOR BRANDING™

Not long after we opened the doors of our agency, we were invited to pitch an account that was—to be perfectly honest—way above our pay grade. It's not that we didn't think we could do the work, but we were still relatively new to the scene and were going up against larger, more established firms.

After several weeks of preparing for the meeting, we arrived at the client's downtown headquarters to make our presentation. Upon arrival, we were ushered to the top floor and into a spacious boardroom where the president sat waiting.

As soon as we entered, it was immediately clear that the man sitting at the head of the table was the one we were supposed to meet with. He was the first to speak, skipping over formalities and introductions and plunging right into his first question: "So, tell me, why should I hire you?"

Now, having participated in countless meetings with studio heads, celebrities, and media giants, this was by no means my first rodeo. But for some reason, his question gave me pause. Did we really never take this into consideration? Had we not taken the time to formulate our own promise behind our brand?

As I began to answer his question, a phantom wall behind the president slid open and a stern-faced butler emerged. He carried a silver tray that included eight almonds, four apple slices, two lemon wedges, and a cup of steaming coffee. Seriously, it was like a classic scene from a James Bond movie, right before James gets dropped into a pit of sharks.

 **Michael:** Okay, so this part of the story doesn't really have anything to do with the outcome of the meeting or what we learned from it, but it remains one of my favorite stories. Fortunately, we were able to provide enough reasons for him to hire us, and it ended up being a rewarding experience for both parties.

What we learned from that experience was that we needed to find a better way of explaining our process. A way of communicating not only the importance of branding, but how we were able to incorporate our own unique branding principles into traditional and more accepted methods of advertising. Sure, we had an understanding of this internally, but we needed to develop something that would also work externally.

This would not only help potential clients understand what we did and how we did it, it would also provide a consistent roadmap for us to follow as our team grew, covering everything from corporate brand assessments to complete rebranding initiatives.

What we needed was a process, and what we came up with was:

RAZOR BRANDING™

He Said: How We Make Brands Razor Sharp

Having a strong and successful brand is not magical, but the results can be. It comes from an understanding of who your audience is, what you do best, and how to deliver on your promise in a consistent manner. Once you're able to answer these questions, you can develop messaging that speaks directly to those who most need to hear it.

Whether we use Razor Branding from start to finish, or simply in principle, thinking about the audience and their brand choices helps our team craft strategies and messaging systems that motivate behavior. We like to refer to this as "changing the conversation."

Jaci: By changing the conversation, we're able to clearly define the brand promise of a company within any given industry. In doing so, consumers can easily understand how a particular product, service, or company can enhance their lives.

In the end, the desired outcome for all marketing and advertising initiatives is to promote loyalty and eventual advocacy for your brand—and the only way to accomplish this is to lead creative with research, consumer insight, and strategy.

So, what exactly is Razor Branding and how does it work? Glad you asked.

Razor Branding permeates all levels of marketing, advertising, and digital and social media, giving us a unique advantage in first identifying our client's target audience and then developing messaging, strategies, and creative that builds awareness, loyalty, and eventual advocacy.

Razor Branding accomplishes this by changing the conversation to better position companies within their marketplace, regardless of industry, size or location.

The process itself develops brands from the inside out, establishing a series of branded touchpoints that form emotional connections with the consumer. Developing these connections relies heavily on understanding the psychographics of audience behavior—

not just demographic profiles, which rarely tell the whole story.

She Said: The Four Elements

Razor Branding in its most basic form is a strategic brand plan that has four core elements: focus, promise, connection, and harmony.

These elements work to answer the following questions:

- Who are you talking to?
- Why should they pick you?
- What are you trying to say?
- Where should you say it?

FOCUS:
(The Who)

Focus helps define who you are and who your audience is through the use of consumer insight,

demographics, psychographics, and personality profiles.

Focus provides an opportunity to get to know your audience, their thoughts and perceptions, and how you can reach them in their heart, because in the end, that's where brands are formed. In many ways, Focus is also about learning more about who *you* are. It gives you an opportunity to look in the mirror and figure out if you are what you say you are, addressing things like your company culture and whether you're providing the type of environment that produces and encourages success.

Is it easy? No. But the rewards are substantial when you take the time to learn more about your exisiting and potential audience.

PROMISE:
(The Why)

Promise defines that one differentiating and power-fully compelling quality that makes your brand razor sharp—in effect, the promise behind the brand.

If Focus is the who, then Promise is the why. It's also the fifth P after product, price, place, and promotion.

It answers these questions: Why choose *you*? What's your promise to the customer that makes you different from the rest?

To be clear, every successful company, big or small, needs to have a Promise—an attribute or facet it can deliver repeatedly and claim authentically on a consistent basis. That promise is what makes you different, setting you apart from the competition.

Consistent delivery of the promise creates trust.

Trust promotes loyalty. Loyalty leads to advocacy. As a business, attracting advocates should always be a priority—no matter what your industry. Why?

Because you want lifelong patrons who will stay with you beyond the first sale. And you want them to share their experiences and invite others to join.

CONNECTION:
(The What)

Connection establishes your "voice" and messaging that is based on your defined brand promise, making you the preferred choice over the competition.

Connection is all about the what. What are you saying? What message is going to capture the attention of your audience, causing them to not only remember you, but be motivated to take some action? Remember, you'll have a primary target audience who requires one message and a secondary target audience who probably requires something else entirely.

For example, each of these audiences might possess two entirely different personality traits. One may be a Headline and the other a Logo—with each requiring their own approach and unique messages.

That's why it's important to pay close attention to your specific audience types, ensuring that your messaging isn't built within a one-size-fits-all structure.

HARMONY:
(The Where)

Harmony works to identify and develop a series of branded touchpoints that establish trust, connecting with your audience where they live, work, and play.

The fourth core element of Razor Branding is where it all comes together. This component is essential to ensuring that everything you've developed so far will actually be seen, heard, and experienced by those it was intended for.

With so many potential opportunities of where to put messages, we can no longer use the dated philosophy of trying to reach 100 percent of the people with the goal of convincing them 25 percent of the time. Instead, we have to reach 25 percent of the people and convince them 100 percent.

So, instead of trying to be everywhere, you should be present in places where you can be most effective.

PART III: THE FINISHING TOUCHES

CHAPTER 7: CHANGING THE CONVERSATION

I remember it like it was yesterday. The year was 2007, and we were two to three years into our branding evolution. Our business was growing steadily. Razor Branding was earning praise from clients, and we were a good year away from the national financial crash that would cripple most of the country. It was a typical Thursday night, and I was doing my best to get our kids, ages seven, six, four, and three, tucked into bed so I could watch *Mad Men*. Michael had already left for the office by then to catch up on work, and I assumed he'd be watching from there as well.

 **Michael:** She makes it sound like I abandoned her to deal with four kids on her own, but in reality, Jaci and I made a commitment early on to be home at five every day, and it's a principle we've adhered to for almost

twenty years. We also encourage our team at brandRUSSO to practice the same, ensuring that the lines between work and family are never compromised. That being said, Jaci and I often found ourselves cracking open a laptop or heading back to the office after our kids were down for the night, which is why on this particular night I had already left for the evening.

Only half paying attention, I could hear Don Draper interrupt a prospective client in the middle of a pitch, saying: "If you don't like what's being said, change the conversation."

As soon as the last word left his mouth, my phone started blaring: Michael. "Are you watching *Mad Men*?" he asked. In the end, I managed to talk him off the ledge and assure him that no, our office was not bugged. But we did get some joy from hearing a phrase on national TV that we'd been using since 2005—and uttered by Don Draper, no less.

For us, "Change the conversation" is our response to clients who are afraid of change and stick to what is most comfortable—dated messaging, positioning, and media channels that have been around for years. What these people fail to understand is that without some form of change, they'll no longer be able to compete. Sure, you can continue to say the same thing everyone else within your industry does, but that defeats the whole purpose of branding, differentiation, and forming those strong emotional connections we keep talking about.

He Said: Water Is Water; Milk Is Milk

We worked with a regional dairy that produced, you guessed it, milk. Now the problem with milk is that it's a commodity. And commodities are a challenge, because they pretty much function the same, no matter the company or brand. Oil is oil. Water is water. And milk is milk. In the eyes of the consumer, all milk looks the same, costs about the same, and basically tastes the same.

To make things more challenging, this particular dairy was not only similar to every other milk you'd blindly pick out of your grocer's refrigerator, but it was also pricier—without being organic.

Going through our Razor Branding process, we started researching stores to find out who most frequently purchased milk and discovered that the majority of buyers were women. Typically, they fell into one of three buckets. People in the first bucket were buying store-brand milk because it was the cheapest, and milk, to them, was milk—a commodity. If someone in the family had a milk sensitivity or allergy, they opted for the pricier organic brand. To this second group, cost was no issue, because health took precedence over money spent. The people in the third bucket bought the brand they'd known and drank since they themselves were children—which we dubbed the "heritage brand."

Again, the setback for our client was that their product had a price point similar to organic without being organic. In a nutshell, there was no spot in this lineup for our client, no category left to fill. Around and around we went with the research, not really sure how we'd carve out a new niche for the company or warrant its higher price point.

Looking at their competitors' strongholds, or the categories they already owned, we knew we could battle them for a space in the lineup. But doing that would cost a lot of money, all for a lot of risk and slim chances of success. The competitors had already won the hearts-and-minds battle. So how could we change the conversation to find another way in? To find another opportunity to get our name out there?

She Said: It Is, but It Isn't

It was at this point we had to dig deep and go beyond the expected. We had to find a way to Change the Conversation. Instead of trying to finagle a way into one of the established buckets, we decided to create a fourth one: a bucket for emotional connection.

For the most part, parents are typically coffee drinkers or water drinkers, but they're not milk drinkers. The women purchasing milk were doing so for their kids. And there we had it: the differentiation needed to position our client in the marketplace.

More research followed, revealing that middle school is around the time when most kids stop wanting whatever is placed before them and become more vocal about preferences. That's how middle schoolers became our target demographic. Our goal was to identify and recognize kids within this age group for doing great things. We built an entire ad campaign around this concept. Whether it was a student who was a top performer on the swim team or an academically inclined student with a learning disability that overcame great odds or even a student running a lemonade stand to raise funds for a classmate with cancer, these kids could be nominated by schools for different categories of excellence. The community would then vote on the final candidates, and the winners would be recognized in an ad campaign, provided an award and a scholarship, and featured for the category they'd excelled in.

So what's the point of this story? What does it exemplify? It shows how we changed the conversation. How we created a niche for our client and made a space for them in a lineup that initially had no room by changing our message and changing the way people were thinking about a commodity like milk.

People went from saying "Well, I drink this particular milk because that's what I grew up drinking" to "Maybe I'll try this other brand because they seem to be connected to my world in some way."

He Said: There's More to It

My idea of changing the conversation is a little different. It's of course similar to what Jaci said, but from a creative standpoint, to me, changing the conversation means not only that we want to change what's being said or say something differently to stand out, but also that we do so *in an authentic way*. Maybe you present information in a way that's outside the norm. Or maybe you say something to explain what you do in a unique way so it's processed differently. For instance, everyone says they have the best customer service. If you're claiming that too, you sound just like the rest—so changing the conversation would be somehow saying it differently to distinguish yourself.

But how do you do that? Well, what I can tell you from my own experiences is that through quantity comes quality.

You really have to grind out multiple ideas, tons and tons of them, before you get to the good stuff. Just like we had to do with our dairy client.

I learned this from Dutch Kepler, my advertising design professor in college. To be honest, I thought he was the devil back then for what he put us through, but looking back, I owe so much to him for teaching me this concept alone. It has been a key factor in our success, and the continued success of our clients.

Trust me, whoever said there are no bad ideas when it comes to brainstorming was just being nice, but that's kind of the point. You have to go through all of the bad to get to the brilliant. It's a brutal and unforgiving process, but it's essential to finding the answer.

To craft incredible headlines, copy, messaging, and conversation, you have to dig deeper than the initial thoughts that float through the surface of your mind, because chances are the first idea you think of has already been tried and tested.

To get down to the super-unique, creative thoughts, you have to filter out everything that's already in your mind and travel past the noise. If you've come up with something off the cuff, you've probably left the best concepts behind on the table.

Call it changing the conversation, cutting through the clutter, or building an emotional connection. Any way you say it, the point of our milk anecdote is that you have to find an opportunity to separate yourself from the crowd so you can stand apart and compete in a unique way. And that's what the Razor Branding process guides us toward every single time. That's the beauty of Razor Branding and how it works, repeatedly and reliably, for any company, of any size, in any industry, and in any geographic location.

Often when people think about branding, their minds go right to the big-brand names: Nike, Coke, Disney, Apple. But hopefully this story helps illustrate that these principles can be applied at a much smaller level too—you just have to know how to use them to your advantage.

CHAPTER 8: WORD TO THE WISE

We've covered a lot of ground in seven short chapters. We've traced the history of branding, talked about what branding is and isn't, and revealed our trade secret at brandRUSSO—Razor Branding and its principles. Basically, we've covered the main elements needed to help drive your company toward branding success, or at best, help you understand how to better guide and involve yourself when working with a hired professional.

But before we call it a day, let's sum up the most important points you've learned and also sneak in a few final ones we think you might use and appreciate. The goal is that when you turn the last page, you'll feel confident that you have the knowledge and principles you need to create (or hire someone to create) a stunning brand that's ready to compete in today's world, with this chapter offering a birds-eye view to it all.

She Said: Let's Review

MAPPING OUT YOUR APPROACH

Before you start any conversation, know who you're talking to, what they think, and, conversely, what you want them to think. Also brainstorm which vehicles or media channels you should use to reach these people. Without a premeditated approach, the branding process can become obscure and confusing, so we strongly recommend mapping out the specifics before you get deeper into any part of branding.

CONVERSATIONS

In branding, you have to get inside your target audience's mind so you craft messaging that will resonate. And the way to do that is through conversations—conversations with customers and prospects. Once you're inside the minds of these individuals, you'll be impossible to ignore, which is exactly what you want. Conversations are integral, because they help drive dialogue and relationships with your clients.

RELATIONSHIPS

Branding, in a nutshell, is all about building a relationship through emotional connection. But before you get to building the right relationship, you should know that there are actually two relationship types: transactional and relational.

Transactional relationships are all about competing to be the cheapest or most affordable among several competitors. This is when companies differentiate themselves by shaving profit margins or launching year-round sales. Sure, this tactic works—until your competition knocks a nickel off and, all of a sudden, you're not the cheapest anymore.

Remember, more often than not, people don't buy things because they're the cheapest. For example, it's not the least expensive cars that sell every day or the cheapest linens being added to shopping carts. We buy for emotional reasons, or because we've had some experience that's convinced us that a particular product or service is superior to the rest. Usually, we even purchase one company's item over its competitor's because of how that particular company makes us feel.

Instead of being transactional, we must strive to be relational. But how do you achieve that? By building a relationship. The principles of Razor Branding are what will help you establish what that relationship will be about.

Essentially, to get started on the right track, you should ask yourself these questions:

WHO ARE YOU?
WHO IS YOUR AUDIENCE?
WHAT ARE YOU ABOUT?
WHAT IS YOUR PROMISE?

Building a relationship means training your team to ask compelling questions so that you're no longer selling customers at a certain price point, but instead promoting things they need and products they could benefit from.

When you focus on being relational, people will drive across town to shop your brand. They'll trust you, which means they'll pass up less expensive and more convenient options without pause to honor your relationship based on that trust. They'll be loyal to you. Then they'll advocate for you. Nurture those relationships and, in the meantime, find ways to separate yourself from customers who have only a transactional interest in you, because those are the ones you'll never profit from.

PROMISE

We've talked about promise quite a bit and seen it reinforced through different principles of Razor Branding. As you're creating your brand, be cognizant of your promise. Make sure it's real, authentic, and true. Why should people choose you? What makes you a better choice over the competition? Once you make that promise, keep it—because your brand is only as strong as that promise.

COMPETITION

Competition is inevitable. But competing means being able to change the conversation and stand out uniquely from the crowd.

People are sometimes apprehensive when they hear those words, because they think standing out means sounding like you're at a monster truck rally. But you don't have to go to extremes to establish an emotional connection; you don't have to go to extremes to stand out. Standing out just means being authentic and being you in that special way that only you *can* be.

We've seen businesses try to stand out the wrong way, often in a manner that's detrimental to the brand. They don't follow the promise behind the brand or stick to its core principles—and when that happens, people sense the inconsistency. They sense that you're not who you say you are. They sense that you're trying too hard. Because you're being inauthentic, which is the opposite of what you should be striving to be.

On the other hand, when you're authentic, people will trust you. When they trust you, they'll join you.

To stand out, you should ask yourself questions like, How am I different? What mental real estate is mine to own? Think back to how we created a new category for milk or how we created First Bank Fred to help the bank stand out. Answering these questions can yield the degree of creativity and differentiation those companies achieved.

LAW OF ATTRACTION

By now, you know that people do business with people, not businesses. The Law of Attraction takes that one step further to say that people do business with people they're attracted to or *like*. But here's the catch: for people to like you, you have to prove yourself to be human—let the human personality of your brand shine through to customers. Don't treat them like a transaction. Only after you let them know you and discover who you are and what you're about will they feel that instinctive tug toward you.

CULTURE

Your culture defines so much about your brand—much more than people often give it credit for. The way you are inside your company reflects on the outside to customers and prospects. If you claim you love customers and your company is customer-centric, but your staff is never trained to treat each customer with respect and care, what does that *really* say about the culture you practice? More importantly, think about the dissonance that creates in customers' minds about who you're pretending to be versus who you really are. How can you expect that dissonance to help you build credibility or trust in your company? To create a culture that's genuine and rings true, think about what makes your company special, and then build your culture around *that*.

THE LAW OF THE JUNGLE

As humans, much like animals, it's in our DNA to blend in—that's the Law of the Jungle. Think about animals that herd together, like elephants, antelopes, zebras, etc. Why do they do that? What's the benefit? It's simple: they understand that there's safety in numbers. They know that sticking together means it's less likely that predators will target and eat them. When they're out on the plains, grazing on grass, and a predator's up the hill trying to figure out which one he's going to feast on, the mass of them looks like one big creature to him. That predator's plan isn't to target a specific animal in the pack—it's just to get some food in his belly. The most likely to become the predator's prey is the one just off a little to the side or the one in the back near the watering hole, where it can easily be singled out and attacked—all because it didn't effectively blend in with the masses. In other words, the ones hanging solo are most likely to get picked off.

If you think about it, there's little difference between animal and human behavior. I hate to pick on high school girls, but since I've got a house full of them, I know from experience that they're the perfect example. When these girls get to junior high, they start to suddenly sound and look alike, listen to the same music, and follow the same influencers. They become this herd—because that's safest. If you don't believe me, think about that one girl who doesn't fit in with the pack. She's a misfit because she doesn't look, act, or sound like the rest. This often means she gets picked on.

For both humans and animals, being different means making yourself vulnerable to attack and susceptible to danger. Our DNA compels us to blend in from our evolution as animals to humans and then even from humans to business owners. This means that as a business owner, every fiber of your instinct will tempt you to follow the Law of the Jungle: blend in, do what everybody else is doing, and look like everyone else in the industry.

But unfortunately, the Law of the Jungle goes against everything you should be doing if you want to stand out and make a splash in the business world. While as humans we're afraid that being the oddball out makes us the perfect target, in business it's the other way around: when you stand out, people notice you, and that's exactly what you want.

Look around and you'll see that the most successful, influential brands out there all have one thing in common: they've found a way to be distinct, break through the clutter, and change the conversation.

CONCLUSION: THE BIG FINISH

Jaci and Michael:

YES, IT'S WORTH IT.

If you have gotten this far, you're either related to one of us, or are directly responsible for your company's marketing efforts and want to find a better way to drive traffic, increase sales, and improve your bottom line. In today's world of evolving technologies and emerging media channels, that can certainly be a challenge.

We hope we were able to address some of these challenges as well as provide some insight into how to build a stronger, more effective brand. It comes from understanding who it is you're talking to, why they should pay attention, what you should be saying, and where you should be saying it. Sounds simple enough, right?

But in order for any of this to work, you have to find ways to utilize consumer insight to build emotional connections with your audience. As we stated, this is the key to successful branding, and it is the only way to build loyalty and advocacy for your brand.

Unfortunately, companies continue to waste money on ineffective advertising, whether it's the result of poor media-buying decisions, lack of consistent messaging, or an inability to properly connect with their audiences.

With a commitment to changing the conversation, these companies can form messaging systems that easily show how what they provide can enhance consumers' lives.

When your audience begins to trust your brand and think of you before the competition, you'll spend less on convincing them to buy, which will lead to increased sales (as you know, brand-loyal customers tend to buy trusted brands more frequently). The most important takeaway here is that successful branding can help alter consumer behavior.

That being said, branding is not a Band-Aid that can be slapped on a faltering business plan. Nor is it a cure-all for a company whose products or services fail to deliver on its promise. But when correctly developed and used as the driving force for business development, successful branding can elevate companies to the top of their industries and keep them there.

Throughout this book we've touched a lot on utilizing both strategy and creative to develop effective branding solutions. This duality factors into our process and our success as an agency.

One of the biggest misconceptions people have about creativity is that they have none. Truth is, being creative has more to do with problem-solving than being artistic.

At its core, that's the most important element behind any strategic branding effort. When you're able to strategically define the who, why, what, and where, you'll be able to develop creative answers that help influence how you're viewed and perceived.

We want to thank you for taking the time to join us on this journey, and we hope you not only gained some insight, but had some fun along the way.

If you have any questions, want to learn more about brandRUSSO, or would like to discover how we might be able to help you and your business find brand nirvana, reach out to us at any of the channels below. We would love to hear from you.

BrandRusso.com

/brandrusso   /brand_RUSSO

/brandrusso